Hard Jolts of Hope

poems by

Natalia Prusinska

Finishing Line Press
Georgetown, Kentucky

Hard Jolts of Hope

Copyright © 2021 by Natalia Prusinska
ISBN 978-1-64662-698-4 First Edition
All rights reserved under International and Pan-American Copyright Conventions. No part of this book may be reproduced in any manner whatsoever without written permission from the publisher, except in the case of brief quotations embodied in critical articles and reviews.

ACKNOWLEDGMENTS

Poems in this collection have previously been published in *Streetlight Magazine* and *High Shelf Press*.

Thank you Owen for your tenderness and quietude. Of all things, you taught me immediacy & joy, so much joy.

Thank you Asia for your support and uncategorical love. You kept the apartment livable while I selfishly read and wrote.

Publisher: Leah Huete de Maines
Editor: Christen Kincaid
Cover Art and Design: Caramurú Baumgartner

Order online: www.finishinglinepress.com or amazon.com

Author inquiries and mail orders:
Finishing Line Press
PO Box 1626
Georgetown, Kentucky 40324
USA

Table of Contents

Intensities 1
How I Think We're Like Rhubarb 2
Needless Acts of Violence Against Time 3
Growing Pains 4
Commonwealth 5
Time of 6
Microeconomics 7
I Am so Tired I Keep Forgetting to Sleep 8
Long Distance 9
Non-act 10
Deadhead Today 11
I Am an Edge to Grasp, Not a Body to Hold 12
Just Shy 13
Visiting My Father After 5 Years 14
Carrier 15
Back of the Mind 16
Outside the Giant Loop 17
Fireweed 18
A Distant, Middle-aged Fire 19
How to Handle Indecision 20
Owning a Fork 21
"Hey, It's Been a While" 22
Negotiations 23
Geese 24
So Close 25
Units of Measure 26
Over-indexed 27
Tough Love 28
Temporary Opening 29
The Licit Love of a Couple in Full Swing 30
Late Start 31
Prone 32
Peace Is a Slippery Bastard 33
All Things Said and Done 34

Experienced radiologists who evaluate chest X-rays as "normal" or "abnormal" contradict themselves 20% of the time when they see the same picture on separate occasions.

DANIEL KAHNEMAN

Intensities

I once had a big-bellied affair,
a grand lust bracketed
by change.
I was once blood held upright
in an electromagnetic field,
constantly being shocked alive.
Once a body roped to other bodies,
caught where the land
drops steeply at 10,000 feet.
In the summer of '06, I shattered the evening
in nineteen places,
hot oil and blood hitting kitchen tile.
Have you ever watched a Sheephead
turn an urchin over
and break its spines?
We are violent in the ways afforded us.
In the case of sex, it comes down to control.
Who sticks whose fingers
in whose mouth?

How I Think We're Like Rhubarb

The day I mooned the neighborhood kids
I ran home and
unscrewed the last lightbulb in my room
to listen to myself
grow faster in the dark.
I crooked my head, listening
for the snaps and pops
of my 13-year old body.
My skin thinned like cheap oil.
I didn't extend but fissure.
Holding a night light, I sat down
and counted all the places
where the light came in funny—
no break yet big enough to see what's inside.

Needless Acts of Violence Against Time

We're different. You slap an orgasm on me and go to sleep.

I squat by the window clutching today against my chest.

History, an old, cataracted mutt, whines softly

in the corner of the room. I shush her,

keeping an eye out for any hint

of light in the street, an ambush of drunken rays firing anywhere,

short lines of light standing on the head of the Earth like flyaways.

I will not let today be another victim of tomorrow.

Your hand reaches out from the other side of the bed to turn off your alarm.

I whisper, "Stay with me. Please, stay with me."

A flash. Nothing. Not even a scream.

Growing Pains

A boy sits next to me on the subway and writes the word "seeds". I start to mouth the word just as he closes the notebook and exits through the door of the R train, each letter wrenched from my mouth like a tooth: the first s, then a pair of e's, a d dragged in blood, and the last s carrying a trailing nerve through my mouth.

I see a man on the edge of the platform take out his marker and write slowly, "Too sorry to write," on the dirty, tiled wall. Oil slicked on a duck. He drags the side of his hand through the ink as he writes. I read it aloud, the letters disintegrating in my mouth like sucking candy.

Think about it. The sound of a letter can break like an aging spine; shrink down to a short sound like a deep sob breaking into a hiccup.

Sometimes it takes years to feel the fullness of a thought.

Commonwealth

I almost forgot the connection
between common and wealth,
but then you said you also wanted
to be rich as fuck.

Time of

men carrying children out of gunfire
like trying to carry all the groceries in one run.
Time of source-less dark that moves at will.
Time of unease—
the wet smell of our past forcing us up.
I snorted the purple powder
even after we all watched B have a stroke, face
slipping like soap or a dream.
Time of TV news
shifting
like a fly onto bloodier things.
Time of disbelief, then belief, resonance.
Slack jaw, then motion.
Time of sustained bursts
like trying to have sex
after carrying a 150-pound grate
up six flights of stairs.
Countdown to the recrudescence of it all.
Orgasm to not.
Time of changeover. Surgency.
The first big mistake of a generation followed by a war.

Microeconomics

Our loosely engineered lives give,
and we fall into other lives.
Under a microscope
I watched small decisions hesitate
& split & split again
as I tried to shout directions
at the moments milling.
By now, the small decisions
are mostly done
like a blasting cap placed on an undocumented explosive.
I hold myself back.
Every small decision we make
is a fraction of the history behind it.

Send Your Love

For a long time
the whole love scheme was a cash grab,
and I wanted in.
I almost got caught
stuffing wads of you in my bag
before running out the backdoor
of a gas station in Waco.
I tried to grab just enough
to make it a few good years alone
if I spent the memories carefully.
Turns out they're flimsy as hell.
Like Listerine strips
that melt before you even close
your mouth around them.
I'm already almost out
so if you could,
send your love.

Long Distance

Origen thought the sun can sin,
and though I'm not the religious type,
on mornings I woke up without you
I tended to agree.

I admonished the sun
to look equally upon the world,
the fixed light
breaking the integrity of our time;
one side of the Earth always
neglected by the sun.

For as long as I could I loved you.

Non-act

I remember my son once spotted
a still-blind leveret
in the stalks of uncut grass
and waited until I turned around
before he crushed it underfoot.
And recently, I heard my neighbors
talk about a cat
found slung like a pair of sneakers
over the rafters in the old bowling alley.
The blood on his jacket sleeve
formed a ring
like a cocktail glass dipped in salt.
It stung my chiffon blouse, though
I still wore it to breakfast the next day.
And when Sean's mom came to the door
and smiled and said,
"Kids, am I right?",
what else was there to do but nod?

Deadhead Today

Remove the spent flowers
of yesterday.
Empty memory
like a foreclosed home;
the old tenants standing by the door,
all their things in a pile by the road.
Tag the house
with "nothing left to steal".
Drive off with Jim Jones playing loud,
telling yourself, *Tomorrow will be safer.*
The next memories you'll want to keep.

I Am an Edge to Grasp, Not a Body to Hold

The rain outside is a mile long.
I can hear clapping and choir
coming from the church behind us.
My lover taps out a fire
in a potted pothos
after putting out incense in the dirt.
The soil is a smooth finish
on the Earth.
It is fine hair
that doesn't hold the shape of curls,
though the fire almost crept up the leaves
like a Sunday
already hooked by the week.
I liked when we were kids
and still stuck our hands in things.
My lover leaves
after we fight about not wanting
to love new people.
I reach into the potting mix.
Was the blazing Earth here? Or here?

Just Shy

Capers picked late, fruit falling open
like robes,
pickled to survive
anything said twice sounds forced
coke cut on the toilet paper dispenser, licked
from your finger right when the party ends
the night sky pulling itself through a hole
in the cloth of the year
pulsing like a sea nettle
She kisses me unsmiling, black tea on my breath
Her kiss packs light

Visiting My Father After 5 Years

He gave me a jar of jam sealed with heat and wrapped in old towels. I placed it carefully in my suitcase between the new clothes and carried it home. I walked into my empty apartment, immediately unpacked the jar and placed it on the counter. I tried to open it, but couldn't. I turned the jar on the counter, every quarter-turn hitting the metal rim with the blade of a knife. I tapped the edge of the jar against the floor, accidentally breaking the tile in one spot. It still wouldn't open. I grabbed the jar and ran it under hot water, thinking that would help; then twisted the sealed lid until I heard a pop. I looked down, at first confused at the still-sealed jar of jam, and then after a moment, I noticed my wrist like a knotted tree. It grew, the way I wished azaleas would, in front of me. I didn't know what to do next, how to wrap my wrist, or who to call. I walked around holding my wrist out in front of me, cupping the air around it. I grabbed the jar with the insides of my forearms, thrust it into the fridge, and texted my mother, "He frced me to openn my3self." She said, "Forgiveness can be exploited too... I'm on my way." Waiting for her to pick me up and drive me to the hospital, I felt like I was ten again, and she was rushing home from work to check that I was still safe.

Carrier

I am not
the wind picking
up the scent
of crushed lavender
and carrying it
through your window.

Only ever a lover,

I do not know
how to
bring change
to a body
without touching
it.

I tell him,

"I can offer you only
the probability of love."

Remind him of the fading brightwork
of our bodies,
orgasms unachieved.

In a last swing,

I find desire
starting so strong
I almost give up.

Back of the Mind

I wish I didn't throw love like food,
excited I can make something happen.
I'm tired of color. Exaltation.
I want a hot cup of water & dirt for a yard.
Hear me out. This time
you won't even know I'm in your life.
Give me the jobs of love no one wants.
I'll work hard.
I'll love you so quietly
you'll sleep right through me.

Outside the Giant Loop

I'll tell my favorite daughter about us.
How we lived together for years
in civil violence,
and then deleted everything
like the flash drive of porn I used to watch
before all the therapy.
How we panicked
and called the cops on ourselves
in the middle of the damn afternoon.
Or how I told lies back then
still small enough
to be convulsed by your throat.
I'll tell her how standing
in the Charles River reservation
I couldn't stop touching your face
despite the pandemic
so we passed the fire into love, then joy, then—
How the doors opened inward,
and we gave the world nothing.
And then I'll let her make her own decisions.

Fireweed

I sit in our field,
full of one thing or another,
and suck on fresh rose hip,
deep red beads meant for tea
Bright coneflowers grew uninterrupted
before the fire,
covering the view like dust
Now, we have fireweed
I identify more with fireweed
It grows plentiful where once
there was something better

A Distant, Middle-aged Fire

Like how I tell the waitress to keep the rest,
it was better to hand myself over than to wait for change.
To rush into decisions
like I was drunk, next in line for the bathroom,
and the stall door just opened.
To suck the years dry like a middle-aged sun, so there's no reason to
return.

How to Handle Indecision

\ Take a soft wipe to it nightly.
\ Repack and smoke it from a cheap, glass bowl.
\ Degauss it.
\ Give it a less fitting name.
\ Leave it unattended in the middle of a Populist riot.
\ Expose it to elemental mercury.
\ Flush it of toxins.
\ Timebox it.
\ Chuck it in a trash fire behind a shopping center.
\ Track it with embedded laser particles.
\ Run it through the wash until it's lost its color.
\ Massage it clean with microcurrents.
\ Ignore it.
\ Call it so often it stops listening.
\ Release it into the bloodstream.
\ Raise it to hunt anything half its size.
\ Open it with unintended harshness.
\ Manipulate it into thinking violence is a temporary attractant.
\ Distract it with soft lighting.
\ Suggest a lighter sentence.
\ Leave it and most of your possessions in a small coastal town.
\ Cheat.

Owning a Fork

Owning a fork was once a sign of opulence,
an intermediary between yourself & the dead pig
cooked slowly over the fire.
We bought a new set of utensils
for the apartment last week
though we didn't *really* need them.

When I was in high school
I couldn't afford pads, so I rolled toilet paper
between my legs to stop the bleeding.
You see, it's easy
to forget absence when it's gone–
the thousand-leaf flower of memory.

Objects are ruthless in open space.
I look around our place
and count all the things we never use
like the box of glassware set aside for dinner parties.
I don't know if we'd ever sell all of our things
and leave our home,
convenience being the greatest diffuser of opinion.

"Hey, It's Been a While"

I can never eat
the whole moment in one sitting,
so I throw on
a faded thought of you
and stand at the kitchen window,
the sky bigger
than my eyes can see.
I admit,
I often leave my memories
to dry by the pool
and forget to bring them in
before the rain.
Did I tell you?
Last Fall, I tried rewilding a hawk,
and it came back
smaller than I remembered it.
I forgot to write down it's wingspan
& the Spanish
you tried to teach me, how long ago?
Each year is another line
on the vision test
I can hardly see from this distance.

Negotiations

It's simple. We'll rub off our fingerprints,
buy new clothes at Savers.
I'll have the World Conservation Union
declare us extinct
while you clean the hair from the vacuum
and change our numbers. Don't forget
to cut down our favorite trees.
This time next year
no one'll know how to reach us.
We'll buy in cash,
get tattoos to cover our bodies,
make new friends
who like to get drunk on Shōchū and ski
on the weekends. One night,
I'll call my ex from a new Thai place
in Lower Queen Anne   and surprise myself
by crying.
Remember how I told you
peppers change color as they ripen?
My hair will grow back darker,
and you won't like it nearly as much, and
our apartment will get to be too small
for our things.
The commute, too far—
all this trouble
just to short ourselves a quiet year.

Geese

They know I am afraid,
hissing at me like a crowning truth
I can't avoid.
I take a wide circle around them,
nauseous from two beers.
I tell myself I am still young enough
to lie convincingly about the future.
I graft to the branches new thoughts,
focus on your hand,
the light welling around us, unseated,
roaming the river for what's left,
late-blooming lilacs
forgotten by the season.

So Close

I used to store your heart
in the mini fridge next to my bed
along with the probiotics
I always forgot to take.
In some cases, you have to break a tooth
and take it out piece by piece
to keep your teeth
from overcrowding your jaw.
Like how you pull
at the week until it's a month, a year.
Some nights
I pass by thoughts of you
and catch myself
placing my keys between my knuckles.
Still others, I go to sleep slowly,
happy and aware.

Units of Measure

I sit on my mother's porch
cutting up time in 10-minute intervals
like reminding yourself
love was only one person ago.

Over-indexed

I read somewhere Walter Benjamin's son
thought everything wet was a kiss.

I move my face closer to the mirror to floss my teeth—
spraying the polished beryllium with a kiss.

My pad is kissed with blood.

I change it before heading out to clean street-snow from our cars.
Outside I am loved down to my skin.

I later trade my kissed clothes for something I'd forget wearing around you.

For the longest time I thought all unspent energy was *passion*.

Tough Love

Our love is
high-energy collisions between particles
of ordinary matter.
It's the ability to draw inaccuracies
like a perfect circle.
Our love's plastic in a landfill,
slightly degraded
but there.
Our love
tears holes in our thoughts
until they're all unwearable
like a child pulling at the necklaces
around your throat.
Our love is a marvel.
It's not free of uncertainty or change.
Our love is 1000 times worse
in the evening
after a long day of distraction.
It's not the choice we made.
Our love, by God, is.

Temporary Opening

The Catalpa tree in his parent's yard
panics and overgrows,
as the low branches steal water from the crown
like how, growing up, my mother stole money
from the stash hidden under my porcelain shoes,
poor regardless.
Here in New York
he wipes love from my face
as we step out of the barn
to watch 10,000 moths
suddenly come out of the pitch
and fly into the fire,
garden edited,
the night caught without its legs shaved—
all triumphantly perfect.

The Licit Love of a Couple in Full Swing

I burn the morning a little longer
before inhaling it,
suck in freshly peeled air.
Let it burl my lungs. It hits different.
Back in bed, I stroke your cock
until it grows frustrated
and blurts out the next thought
that pops into its head.
We make nothing of the hours
staring at our neighbor's field,
held back by chain-link fencing.
In the evening, I take a long, hot shower
and toss the rest of the day out.
It never tastes as good re-heated anyway.

Late Start

The sun cheaps out on the spread again. I smile smally and nip at the partial light, our sheets wrinkled like baklava. My comfort is occasioned by our things: the books of Sontag and Barthes like stacked rings on the dresser; a rice bag, cold and useless by my left leg; our pants let loose in the courtyard of our bed. You don't clock into the morning for another hour. By then everything is already so close—the two of us lying in the front row of the day. I am three heart attacks behind my father, we both are, and it shows—just look at us smearing the day with knife-fulls of sleep. I sneak off to spike the air with lavender oil, and soon we're too drunk to leave.

Prone

I sit in a warm bath,
cleaning the catheter between my legs,
tapping lightly
at the rip cord.

Blood floats like jellyfish,
all sun and mucus.

My hair grows unopposed.

I make my way to the bedroom,
hand cupped
below the incision to keep from
leaking on the carpet.

I am barred from my body,
and yet

he still asks to see me naked.

Peace Is a Slippery Bastard

Guilt is a dry thunderstorm—heaviness emptied, only to be returned again. Every day I'm trying to earn my peace. \\ I stare out at your parent's yard, the night clarified of birds, blissful from the silence. Inside we listen to Johnny Cash's version of "Solitary Man" while microwaving leftovers. I write in my phone: a lie is a poorly done cover of a song. \\ As a kid, I stained my hands with methylene green, and it took months for my skin to wear away. \\ O, I'm close to telling you how terrible I am. \\ I look at the pictures of our recent engagement; laughter is joy shedding. Already it's another day. \\ I clear the bed of my debts and doubts, and lay next to you, a stolen copy of Camera Lucida in hand. The clouds at our window disperse light evenly. I pocket the un-used shadows just in case.

All Things Said and Done

The city is heels up waiting for the heat, and Night,
Night is black-out drunk
before we even leave the apartment.
Blood pours out of me like vodka down a luge.
I wipe a slap of blood from my leg,
strap a fresh pad to my underwear, and head outside.
I forget to watch the hours again, and they make a mess of time.
So I cache my desire in texts:
"Next weekend let's recreate Elvis Presley's
last performance of Unchained Melody. Slur, shock, awe."
Or, "Maybe we should try anal."
Or maybe I should finally tell you
about the time I accidentally taped a new smell over yours. Start with
a smaller instance of the problem.
That's what my sister tells me.
Night is yelling at me from the top of the stairs.
Blood slips from my underwear. I touch the side of my leg, checking
for wet spots.
Outside a one-woman street band encrypts life in song.
I stop to sit in the park near the station, light a joint of this world, and
look around.
Not bad for God's first time, don't you think?

www.ingramcontent.com/pod-product-compliance
Lightning Source LLC
LaVergne TN
LVHW041555070426
835507LV00011B/1089